Messages from Mars

by **Loreen Leedy** and **Andrew Schuerger**
illustrated by **Loreen Leedy**

Holiday House • New York

Library of Congress Cataloging-in-Publication Data
Leedy, Loreen.
Messages from Mars / written by Loreen Leedy and Andrew Schuerger ; illustrated by Loreen Leedy.— 1st ed.
p. cm.
ISBN-13: 978-0-8234-1954-8
ISBN-10: 0-8234-1954-1
1. Mars (Planet)—Juvenile literature. 2. Space flight to Mars. I. Title: Messages from Mars. II. Schuerger,
Andrew. III. Title.
QB641.L39 2006
523.43—dc22
2005050267

To the first person who sets foot on Mars

The authors wish to thank Dr. Hap McSween of the Planetary and Earth Sciences Department at the University of Tennessee and Dr. Chris McKay of the Planetary Science Division, NASA Ames Research Center, for commenting on the text and sketches prior to publication.

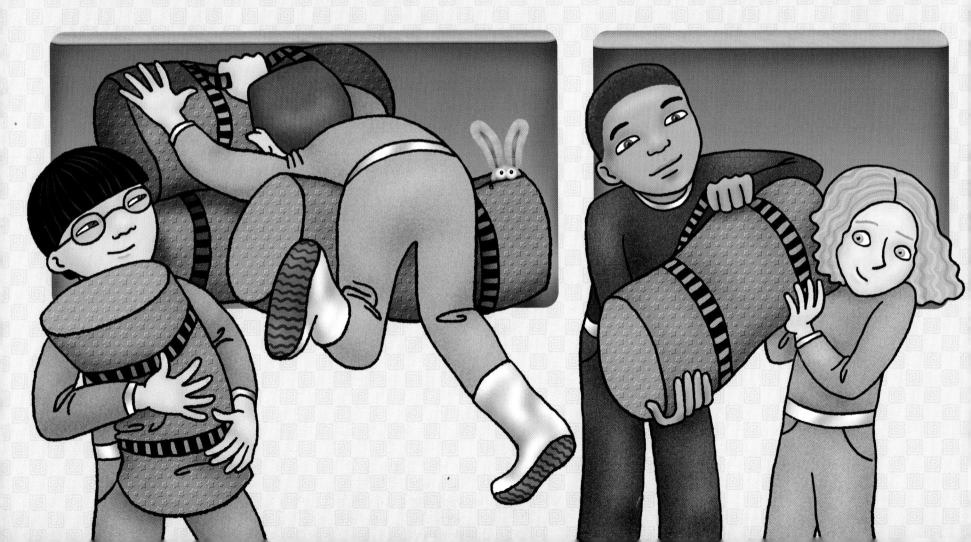

To:Fernandos999 From: ShootingStar

Dear Mom, Dad, Maria, and Ricky,
We are blasting off soon— I'M SO EXCITED! Can you
believe we're really going to Mars? Here are pictures
of everybody going on the trip:

Dr. L   Irisa   Pete   Yong   Spike   K27   Me

Our team leader, Dr. Lucas, is really smart. Irisa
likes butter pecan ice cream as much as I do. K27 is
our hoverbot. He (it?) can do some amazing things.
Gotta go. I miss you already!
OXOXO Elena

Send
Delete

3

COCKPIT CAM

To: K_12marsnews From: F_Lucas   June 1, 2106
Dear Teachers and Students all over Earth,
The pilots have just told us our spacejet *Vision* is ready to go. I wish you could all come with us. Instead, we'll send you photos and tell you what's going on every step of the way. That's because we all have a new FlexAble laptop with a built-in camera and microphone. The laptops can fold up to fit in our pockets! It's time for us to get buckled up now, so farewell.
To Mars!
Dr. Fara Lucas

To: Superteach From: marzguy
Dear Mrs. Morgenstern,
We're in space! When you put my name into the Go2Mars contest, I didn't think I'd really win. It will only take us three days to get there because this Korlin fusion drive spacejet is so fast. Just think...a hundred years ago it would've taken us six months to get to Mars.

Earth looks beautiful from space. It'll be cool going from our watery world to the dusty desert planet of Mars. It's going to be so AWESOME!!! Thanks again!
Your student,
Dillon "Spike" Sheriden

P.S. Here's a photo for the school website to show how I look in my helmet. (Just kidding.)

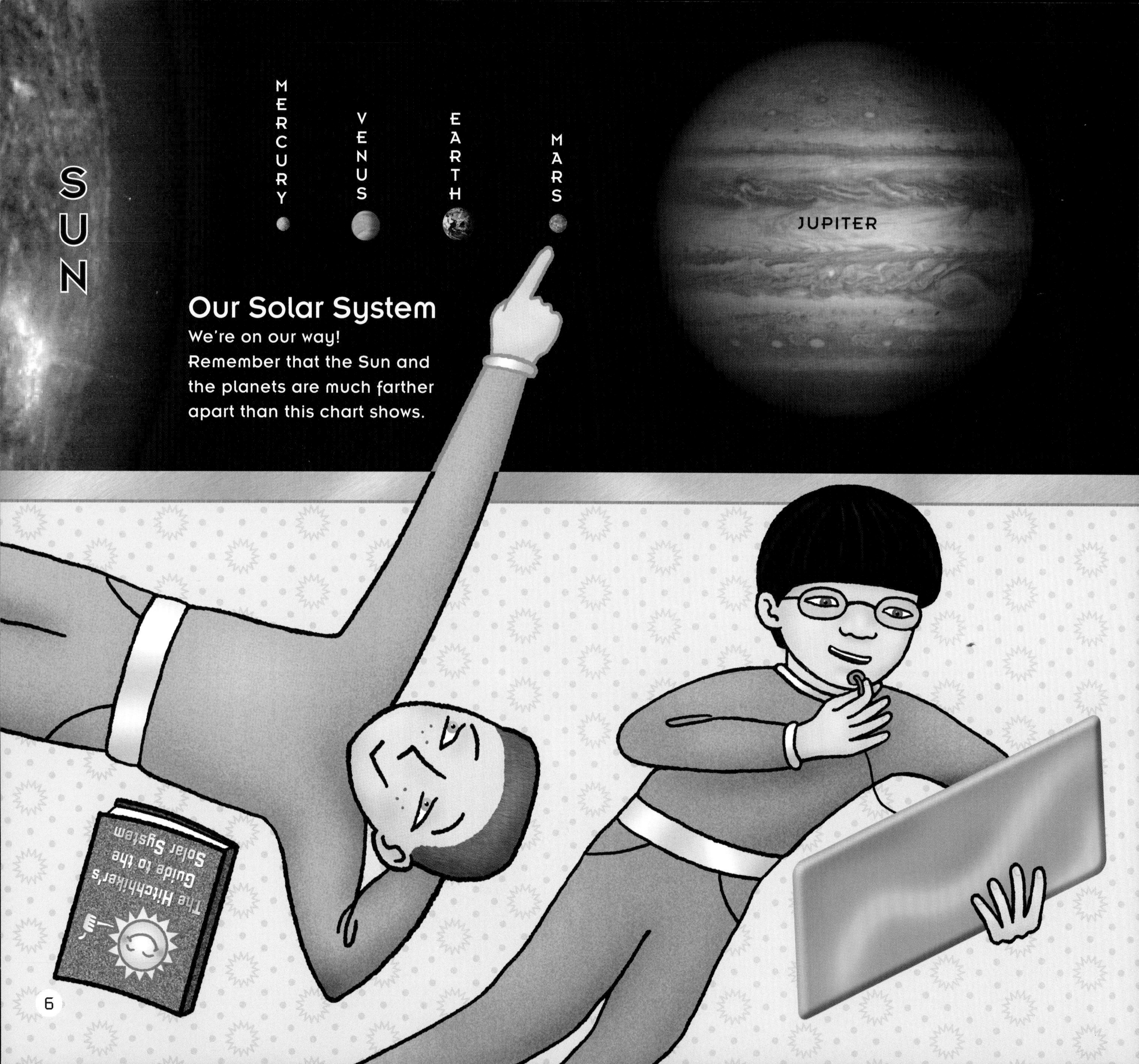

SUN

MERCURY ● VENUS ● EARTH ● MARS ●

JUPITER

Our Solar System

We're on our way!
Remember that the Sun and
the planets are much farther
apart than this chart shows.

The Hitchhiker's
Guide to the
Solar System

SATURN

URANUS

NEPTUNE

To: Chengs10000 From: #1Tiger

Dear Mom and Dad and Chan Juan,

We're learning a lot about Mars before we even get there. Mars is the fourth planet out from the Sun, right after Earth. So we really don't have far to go, only about 90 million kilometers.

The small inner planets (Mercury, Venus, Earth, and Mars) are rocky. Jupiter, Saturn, Uranus, and Neptune are much bigger and are called gas giants. Pluto is different because it's a mixture of rock and ice. I'll write more soon.

Love, Yong

P.S. Can you guess how many planets the size of Mars could fit inside Jupiter?

About 8,474. And about 1,275 planets the size of Earth.

P.P.S. There's no gravity on the ship now, so if we take off our gravity boots, we can float! It's FUN!

Earth

Mars

To: ^B#X6p8 From: K27

** BEGIN MESSAGE **

I am helping the human puppies with days and years. They must learn that one DAY means one rotation of Earth. Earth takes 24 hours to turn around one time.

A day on Mars is called a SOL. One sol means one rotation of Mars. Mars is a little slower than Earth. It takes 24 hours and 39 minutes to rotate once.

Mars

Sun

Earth

Note: not to scale

They must also know that a year is one orbit around the Sun.
1 Earth Year = 365 days
1 Mars Year = 687 Earth days
Mars takes longer to orbit the Sun. It is farther away, so it has a longer trip around.

You and I are programmed to know these facts. But these poor human puppies must learn things. It is lucky I am here to teach them.

** END MESSAGE **

Around the Solar System in 80 Days

To: Jo2 From: ShootingStar

Dear JoJo,

I've got a great idea for people who want to lose weight—go to Mars! If you weigh 100 kilograms on Earth, you only weigh 38 kg on Mars. That's because a smaller planet has less gravity than a bigger one.

There is ZERO gravity on the spacejet. We have gravity boots if we want to stick to the floor, but nobody wears them much, so we float around. Also, there is some goop to hold our hair down. I don't use the goop, because it's funny to see my hair sticking out all over. Maybe I'll send you a picture (or maybe not).
Your friend,
Elena

To: bearhug From: rainbowrider

Dear Simon,

Did you know there isn't much air on Mars? Earth's air is about 100 times thicker. I drew these little air squares to show what I mean.

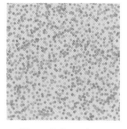

Earth's air

Mars' air is much thinner

Also, the main gases on Mars are different than on Earth. That's one reason why plants and animals from Earth can't live outdoors on Mars. So, the next time you go outside, take a deep breath and enjoy the fresh air!

Bye4now,

Irisa

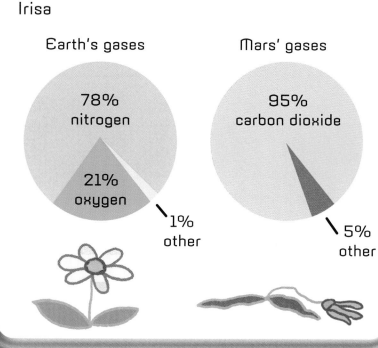

Earth's gases

78% nitrogen

21% oxygen

1% other

Mars' gases

95% carbon dioxide

5% other

To: 680gamer From: rokhound

Dear Melvin,

Mars is a lot colder than Earth. It can get down to -125 degrees Celsius, which is 200 below zero in degrees Fahrenheit. YIKES! Sometimes it can get up to +22°C on Mars, which is equal to +72°F. That's a lot better. Also, it's warmer near the equator, just like on Earth. But we can't wear shorts and sandals outside! You have to wear a space suit to survive.

Stay cool,

Pete

To: Sheridens977 From: marzguy

Dear Mom, Dad, and you rugrats,
You won't believe this, but I almost got into big trouble today. I took off my gravity boots and floated into the engine room. K27 came and pulled me out. While he was in there he found a problem in a rocket thruster.

So I may have saved us from getting stranded on an asteroid! (Just joking.) Anyway, we're almost all the way to Mars—tomorrow is the big day!
Love, Spike
P.S. Don't worry, Mom, the food isn't bad at all. We'll pick up fresh fruits and vegetables at the Mars colony.

To: #2Cheng From: #1Tiger

Dear Chan Juan,

We're now orbiting Mars and we have a fantastic view! The planet has a reddish color because of the iron and other minerals in the rocks and soil. Also, Mars has no blue oceans or green plants like Earth. The poles are white because they are covered with ice. The north polar cap is larger and is made of water ice. The south cap is frozen carbon dioxide and water ice. The polar caps get bigger or smaller as the seasons change on Mars.

Your big brother,

Yong

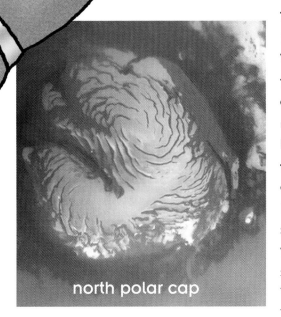

north polar cap

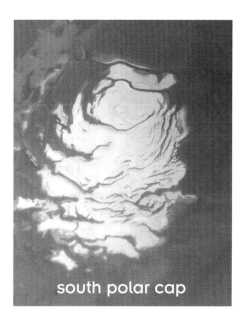

south polar cap

To: K_12marsnews From: F_Lucas

Dear Teachers and Students,

Here are the two moons that orbit Mars. They look like floating potatoes, don't they? Phobos is about twice as big as Deimos, but they both are pretty dinky next to Earth's moon. Phobos is 27 kilometers in diameter and Deimos is 15 km, while Earth's moon is 3,476 km in diameter.

Do you see that big crater on Phobos? It has many more impact craters than Deimos. We can see craters large and small all over Mars from here.

Till next time,

Dr. Fara Lucas

Deimos

Phobos

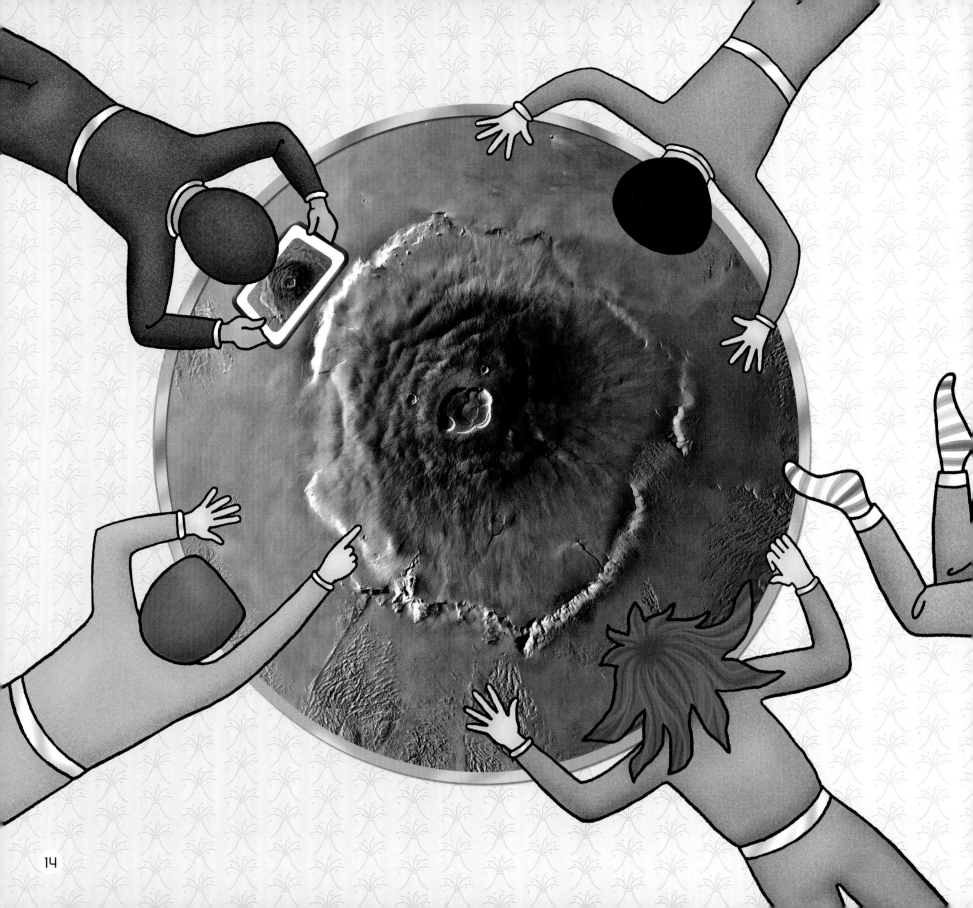

To: SuperOrlovs From: rainbowrider

Hi, everyone! We just flew over Olympus Mons. It is the biggest volcano in the whole solar system. Dr. Lucas says that it was formed by layers of lava. Most of the lava came out of the center opening, which is called the caldera.

It's a very wide volcano with gentle slopes, not steep ones. But it would be very hard to climb to the top. Do you know why? That's because Olympus Mons is WAY bigger than Mt. Everest, the tallest mountain on Earth (see below).

Oops, I'm making a model of a volcano, but I forgot there's no gravity in the spacejet. Lava is going all over the place! Gotta go!

Irisa

caldera

Olympus Mons : 27 km tall

Mt. Everest : 9 km tall

15

To: M+DMason From: rokhound

Hi, Mom and Dad! Have you ever noticed the long mark across the equator of Mars? It's a huge rift valley called Valles Marineris, and it's the biggest canyon in the solar system. The diagram shows that it's as long as the U.S. is wide. It wasn't eroded by river water like the Grand Canyon. Instead, it was formed when liquid rock inside Mars bulged out and ripped open the crust. Isn't that cool?

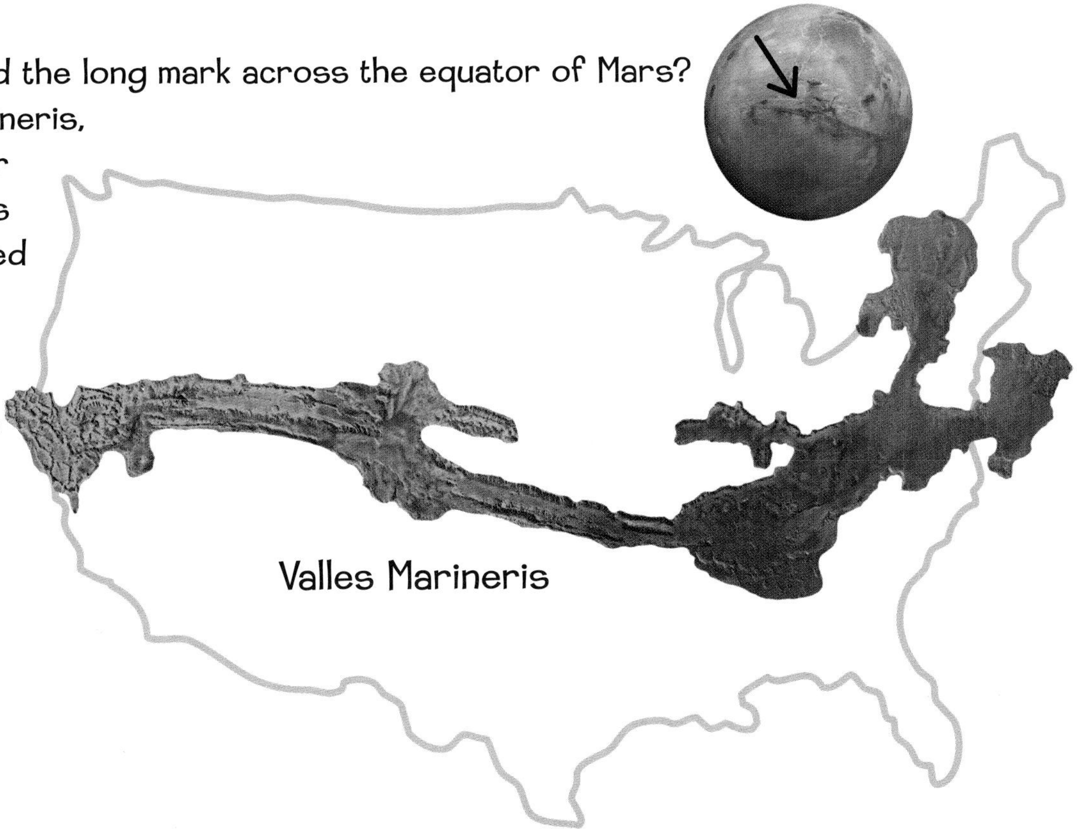

That must have caused a GIGANTIC earthquake. Oops, I mean marsquake. I'm making a model of it with clay on top of a balloon. I would love to see a planet split open like that. From a safe distance, anyway. More later!

Love,

Pete

Valles Marineris

1

2

To: Sheridens977 From: marzguy

Hi, everybody! Did you know that Mars has a lot of wind? Photo 1 shows how it usually looks. Photo 2 shows a global dust storm that is covering the whole planet Mars. Some of the storms can last for three or four months!

3

4

These photos show a dust storm on Mars (3) and a dust storm on Earth (4). They look a lot alike, don't they? But lucky for us, the ones on Earth don't totally cover the planet and keep blowing for weeks and weeks. I hope this wasn't too long-winded for you!
Love,
Spike

1

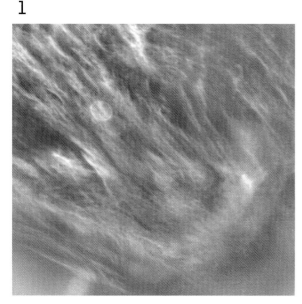

To: Zippydooz From: rainbowrider

Dear Rosita and Ricky,
Where is the water on Mars?
One place to find it is in
the sky. Photo 1 shows thin
clouds made of ice.

The ground in Photo 2 is
covered by a thin layer of
frost. Also, the polar caps
are made mostly of water ice.
But there are no free-flowing
lakes, rivers, or oceans.

2

Guess what Photo 3 is? It's a frozen lake inside
a crater near the north pole. Scientists have
found many clues that show that in the distant
3 past there was much more water on Mars.

4

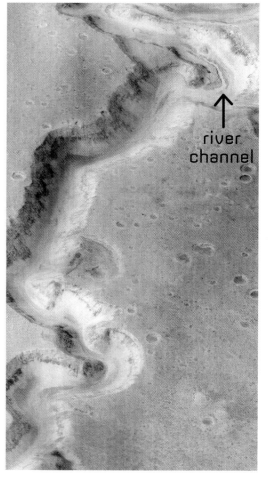

river channel

Photo 4 shows a
deep canyon made
by a river that is
gone now. The arrow
shows the channel
made by the river.
So, where did the
water go? Scientists
will keep studying
Mars to figure it out.

We're getting ready
to touch down!
GOTTA GO!
Your friend,
Irisa

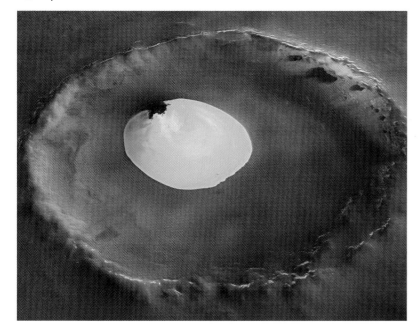

Checklist for EVA
1. Liner
2. Suit   8. Helmet
3. Controls   9. Seals
4. Gloves   10. Air supply
5. B

20

To: #2Cheng From: #1Tiger

Dear Chan Juan,

Our spacejet is on Mars! We're at the site where Viking 1 landed in 1976. There was also a Viking 2 lander that was on the other side of Mars. Each lander had two cameras and a radio to keep in touch with Earth. The landers could detect marsquakes, study the weather, test what the soil is made of, and look for microscopic life. They couldn't drive around, but they did a lot right where they were. I think it's funny that the first photo Viking 1 took was of its own footpad. See?

Speaking of feet, now that we have gravity again, we have to be careful not to trip over all the rocks.

Your big brother,
Yong

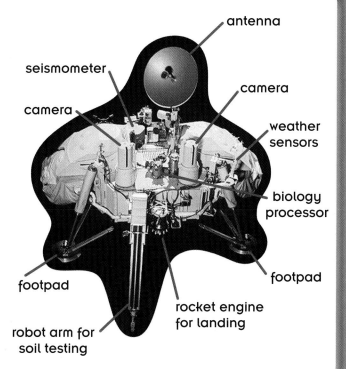

antenna

seismometer

camera

camera

weather sensors

biology processor

footpad

footpad

robot arm for soil testing

rocket engine for landing

To: •8Òjœ8Å From: K27

BEGIN MESSAGE

Humans look for signs of life wherever they go in the solar system. The Viking 1 lander's first experiment to look for life was on July 28, 1976. The lander reached out with its robot arm to dig a trench. Then it picked up a scoopful of soil for testing.

Viking 1 placed the soil into its biology processor. Water and nutrients were added so the microbes (if any) could grow. The results were that some gas formed that could have been made by microbes. At first, it seemed that Viking 1 had discovered life on Mars. Later, most scientists agreed that the gas was created by minerals in the soil. Life might exist somewhere else on the planet. I will stop writing now because we must hurry to the next historic landing site.

END MESSAGE

gas

water

soil

To: bella222 From: ShootingStar

Hi, Anna! We're at the historic site where Mars Pathfinder landed in 1997.

Pathfinder's landing on Mars was so amazing! As the spacecraft entered 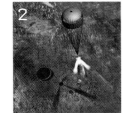 the atmosphere it slowed down to about 1,500 kilometers an hour (photo 1).

Next, the parachute opened. The rockets fired to slow Pathfinder  down some more (2). Then, it turned into a giant basketball! (Only kidding.)

Before landing, big air bags on the spacecraft inflated (3). It bounced up and down for more than a kilometer.

It came to a stop (4), the air was let out of the bags, and the lander opened up. Then, the rover came out. Uh-oh, Spike just fell down, so I have to go help him. Bye!
Elena

Sojourner Rover

The Rock Garden

Pathfinder Lander

To: csagan From: rokhound

Hi, buddy! Everything is still like it was in 1997 at the Pathfinder landing site. This was the first mission to test rocks on another planet to see what they're made of. The first two rocks that were tested are right in front of me. They are nicknamed Barnacle Bill and Yogi. I'm going to add them to my rock collection (with my camera).

This was Sojourner's first step (roll?) off the lander.

The little rover, Sojourner, is still sitting right where it ran out of power after 83 sols on Mars. It traveled pretty slowly, about 1 kilometer an hour. And Sojourner actually drove only 110 meters in all, but it did a great job. Gotta go now to another landing site. Talk to you soon!

Pete

Sojourner at Yogi
July 21, 1997

← Yogi

Barnacle Bill →

P.S. These mountains are called Twin Peaks.

To: Chengs10000 From: #1Tiger
Hi, everyone! We are on the spot where Spirit landed on January 3, 2004. It came bouncing down onto the surface of Mars inside an air bag system (the same kind that Pathfinder used). The lander opened up so the Spirit rover could drive off and start exploring. The lander is still here, covered with dust.
Love,
Yong

whee!

Spirit Rover

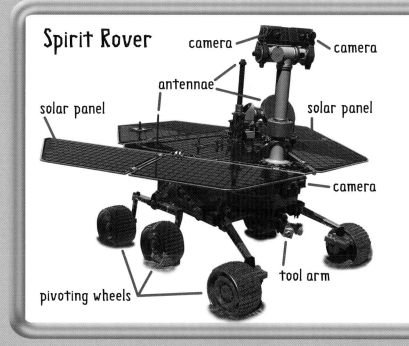

camera — camera

antennae

solar panel — solar panel

camera

tool arm

pivoting wheels

To: Reddogg From: marzguy

The Spirit rover was a robot with lots of special equipment. It had a tool arm that could reach out, several cameras to take photographs, and solar panels to make its own power. I'm taking photos, too, but I'm pretzel-powered (ha-ha)! Anyway, wish you were here!
Your bud,
Spike

1

To: skatergranny From: rainbowrider

Hi, Grandma! You may not want to hear this, but today we saw a rock with RAT holes in it! The letters *R-A-T* stand for Rock Abrasion Tool. Spirit used it to grind into rocks to find out what they were made of. Photo 1 shows Spirit's tool arm drilling its first rock (Adirondack Rock). In Photo 2 you can see the mark made by the RAT. The rock turned out to be basalt. That means a volcano made it. I miss you!
Love, Irisa

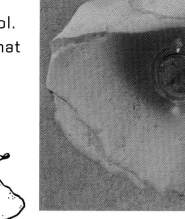

2

To: °hQÅ+»2 From: K27

BEGIN MESSAGE

Do you know what the Spirit rover found? It was salt (see photo). It is not the kind humans put on food. The rover discovered other kinds of mineral salts. Scientists think this area had water billions of years ago. When the water dried up, salts were left behind in crusty layers.

I gave rides to the human puppies up to Lookout Point. They kept saying this funny word: *YEEHAW!* Are you programmed to know what it means? It is not in my memory. Your help needed.

** END MESSAGE**

To: K_12marsnews   From: F_Lucas
Dear Teachers and Students,
As the Spirit rover drove around exploring Mars it made many discoveries. For example, it found magnetic dust. That means there is iron in the soil.

The rover was designed to last for only three months, but it lasted much longer. This picture shows its tracks. And did you know about Spirit's identical twin? It was another rover named Opportunity. We'll go visit that site next. See you there!
Dr. Fara Lucas

To: MendezDE From: ShootingStar

Hi, Stevie and Jackie! We just got to Endurance Crater. It's about 130 meters across and 20 meters deep. It's called an impact crater because it was formed when a large meteor fell down from space. As the meteor hit, dirt and rocks were thrown up and out. They piled up and made a rim around the crater. It's so amazing to be standing here in person.

Your cousin,

Elena

P.S. Spike almost fell in a second ago!

He's lucky that K27 keeps his eyes on him.

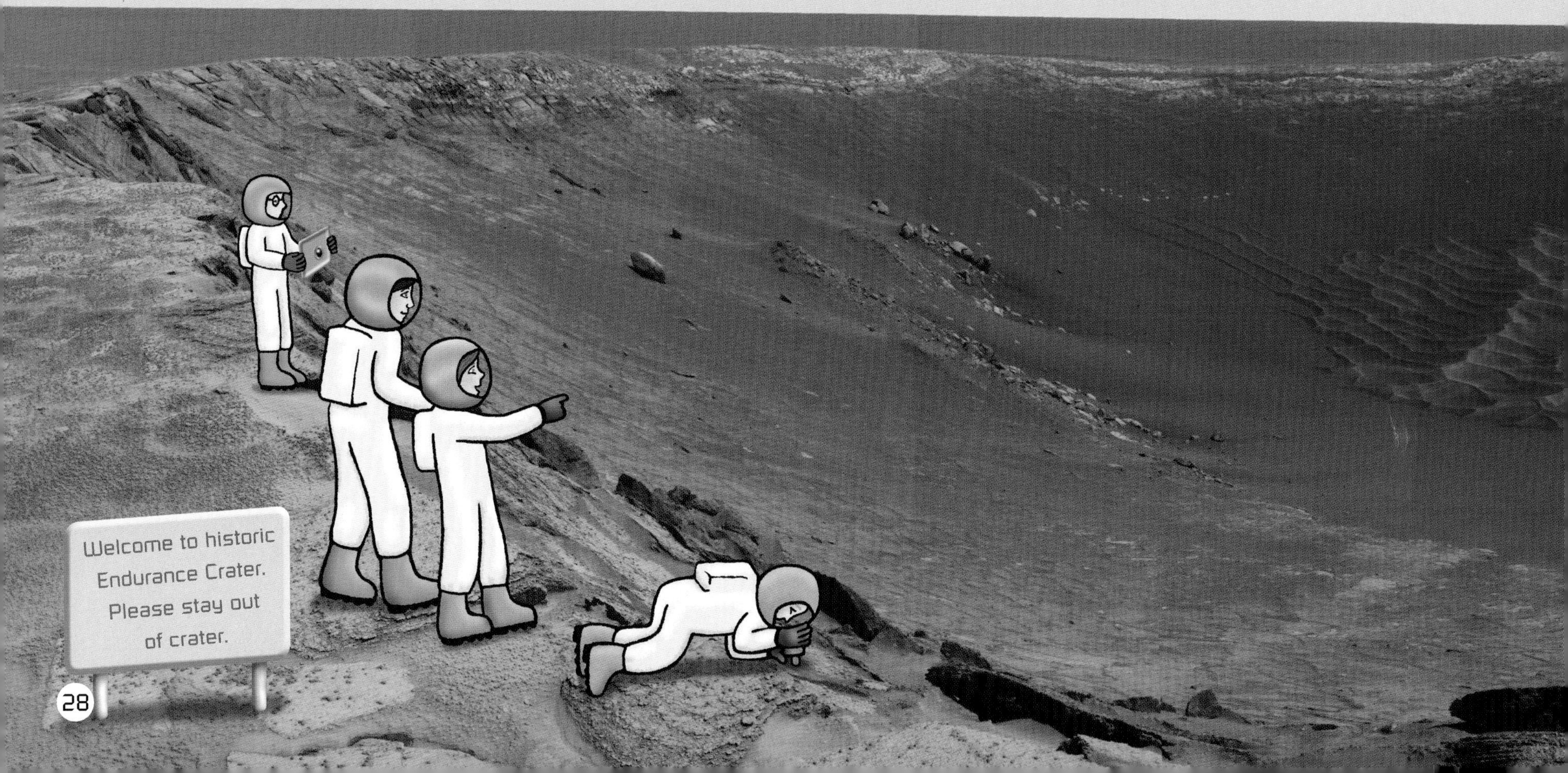

Welcome to historic Endurance Crater. Please stay out of crater.

To: n8 From: rokhound

Hi, Uncle Nate! Guess what the Opportunity rover found while it was exploring? Blueberries! Sorry, but you can't eat them because they're too crunchy. Blueberries are little, hard, round pebbles that were formed in soil where there was water. After a long time (like millions of years), the soil turned into rock. Then, after even more millions of years, the softer rock eroded away. Now the blueberries are lying all over the ground. Talk to you again berry soon!

Luv,
Pete

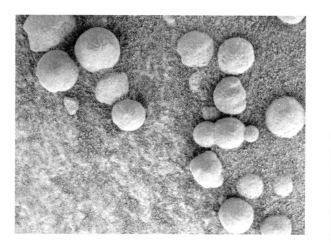

The average size of a blueberry is about 5 millimeters across.

To: bebop From: #1Tiger

Hi, Bo! We have been checking out Endurance Crater. There is an area along the rim called Burn's Cliff. To get a better view of it, we sent K27 down inside and he took a picture for us. You can see thin lines in the rocks, which are layers, sort of like in a birthday cake. They used to be layers of soil covered by salty water. When the water dried up, the salts made the soil layers stick together. After many millions of years, the layers have turned into rock.

Yong

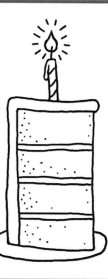

To: soccerqueen From: rainbowrider

Hi, Aunt Zelda! Right now we are flying over part of the giant canyon called Valles Marineris. It's a fantastic view! We've had a great day visiting the historic landing sites of the early missions to Mars. Now we're on our way to the colony. Marsbase Alpha is near the equator, where it's warmer and sunnier. It's also close to underground water. I can't wait to see it. Bye4now!
Love, Irisa

To: Sheridens977 From: marzguy
Dear Mom, Dad, Sean, and Lizzy,
We're inside Marsbase Alpha, and it's amazing!
Fruits and vegetables are all over the place
because the colonists grow most of their own
food here. They even have real blueberries.
We get to pick whatever we want to eat for
lunch. Hey, maybe I could be a Martian farmer
when I grow up.
Love, Spike
P.S. We just saw a dust devil go by the window.
I mean those little whirlwinds that look like
tiny tornadoes. I haven't seen K27 in a while.
Maybe he's still unloading the spacejet. Bye!

35

To: Go2Mars-crew From: K27
BEGIN MESSAGE
Attention, human puppies. This is a time line of Mars Milestones. These historic missions were successful when it was much more difficult to get to Mars. More recent missions will be found in my next message.
Note these codes:

USA: United States of America

USSR: The former Soviet Union

ESA: The European Space Agency
END MESSAGE

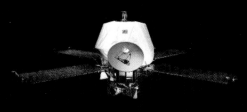

● 1971 Mariner 9 Orbiter   USA
Found Evidence of Water

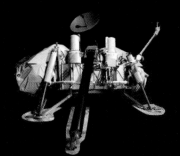

● 1976 Viking Landers 1 & 2   USA
1st to Search for Life

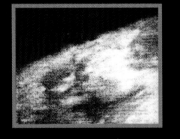

● 1965   Mariner 4   USA
Took 1st Close-up Photograph

● 1971 Mars 3 Lander   USSR
1st Successful Landing

● 1976   Viking Orbiters 1 & 2   USA
Made 1st Global Map

To: K_12marsnews From: F_Lucas
Dear Teachers and Students,
We hope you've enjoyed seeing Mars with us. Maybe you can come someday soon. Just so you know what to pack, here are some fast facts. Earth and Mars are similar in a few ways, but mostly they are very different. We're blasting off in one hour, so see you soon!
Dr. Fara Lucas

	Number of Moons	Distance from Sun	Length of Day
Earth	One	147–152 million kilometers	24 hours
Mars	Two	207–249 million kilometers	24 hours and 39 minutes

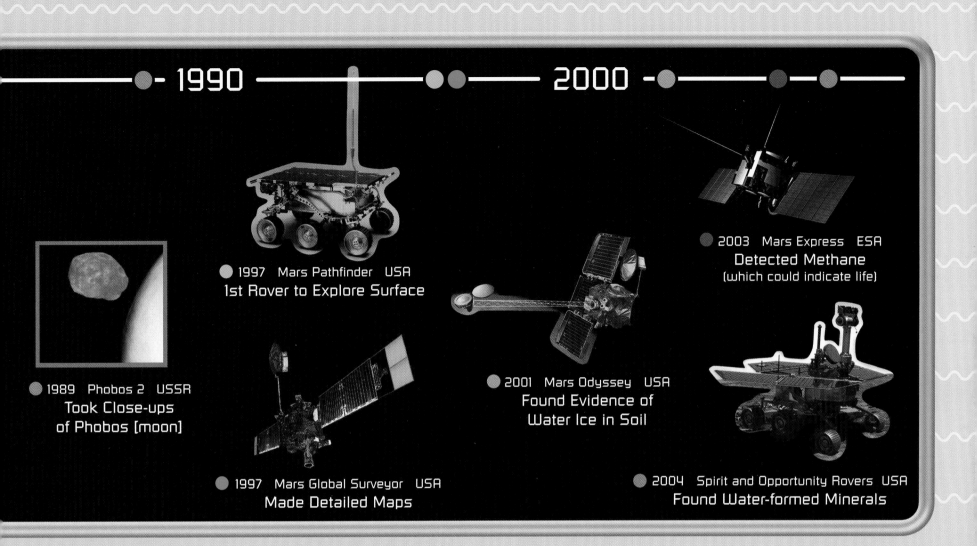

— 1990 — — 2000 —

1989 Phobos 2 USSR
Took Close-ups
of Phobos [moon]

1997 Mars Pathfinder USA
1st Rover to Explore Surface

1997 Mars Global Surveyor USA
Made Detailed Maps

2001 Mars Odyssey USA
Found Evidence of
Water Ice in Soil

2003 Mars Express ESA
Detected Methane
(which could indicate life)

2004 Spirit and Opportunity Rovers USA
Found Water-formed Minerals

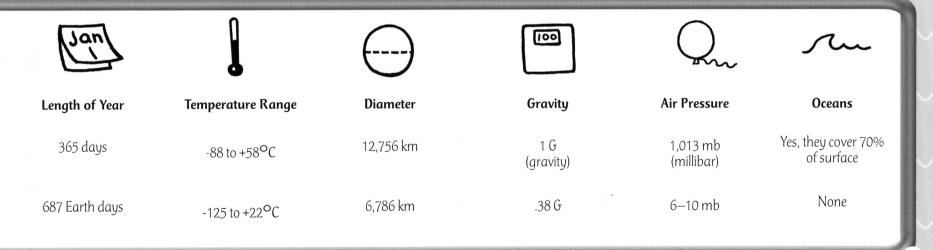

Length of Year	Temperature Range	Diameter	Gravity	Air Pressure	Oceans
365 days	-88 to +58°C	12,756 km	1 G (gravity)	1,013 mb (millibar)	Yes, they cover 70% of surface
687 Earth days	-125 to +22°C	6,786 km	.38 G	6–10 mb	None

More Martian Marvels?

Here are some of the questions that scientists are working on:

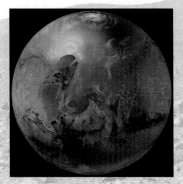

Did Mars ever have an ocean? In the distant past, Mars may have had an ocean in the low-lying areas in the north. This image shows a photo of Mars with blue painted in where the ocean might have been. Signs of an ancient shoreline can be found today.

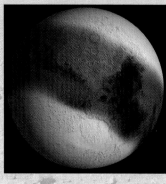

Did Mars have ice ages? During an ice age thick sheets of ice, called glaciers, slowly move across the land. Mars wobbles on its axis as it rotates, which can cause severe changes in its climate. A large part of the planet may have been covered by ice in the past. If so, this picture shows what it may have looked like then. There may be some glaciers on Mars now.

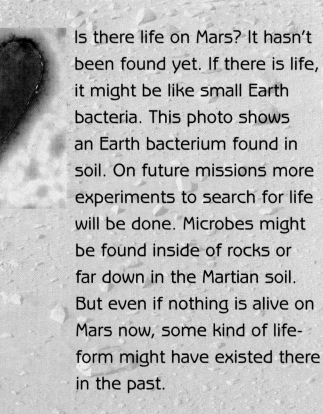

Is there life on Mars? It hasn't been found yet. If there is life, it might be like small Earth bacteria. This photo shows an Earth bacterium found in soil. On future missions more experiments to search for life will be done. Microbes might be found inside of rocks or far down in the Martian soil. But even if nothing is alive on Mars now, some kind of life-form might have existed there in the past.

What can meteorites tell us about Mars? This is an actual chunk of Mars that fell down to Earth. Meteorites from Mars and the Moon fall to Earth fairly often and can be tested in various ways. This one is made of two types of basalt. How do scientists figure out where a meteorite comes from? Find out the answer and many more fun Mars facts at www.LoreenLeedy.com.

Mars Words

atmosphere	the various gases around a planet
axis	the line that runs from the north to the south pole that a planet rotates around
basalt	a dense rock formed by a volcano
blueberries	small, round rocks formed in groundwater
caldera	a sunken area on top of a volcano where the lava came out
carbon dioxide	a gas made of 1 carbon and 2 oxygen atoms
crater	the depression left by a fallen meteorite
diameter	the widest distance across a circle
equator	a circle around a planet exactly between the poles
gas	matter that is not liquid or solid
lander	a spacecraft designed to make a landing
lava	molten rock that comes out of a volcano
methane	a gas made of 1 carbon and 4 hydrogen atoms
mineral	matter that is not from animals or plants
orbit	one trip around a planet or sun
orbiter	a spacecraft designed to orbit a planet
rift valley	a valley caused by a crack in a planet's crust
rotation	one complete turn of a planet around its axis
seismometer	an instrument to detect marsquakes
sol	one rotation of the planet Mars; a Mars day

Metric System

Metric Abbreviations	Metric and English Equivalents	
mm millimeter	1 inch = 2.54 centimeters	1 millimeter = 0.04 (1/25th) inch
cm centimeter	1 foot = 30 centimeters	1 centimeter = 0.39 inch
m meter	1 yard = 0.9 meter	1 meter = 3.28 feet
km kilometer	1 mile = 1.6 kilometers	1 kilometer = 0.62 mile

Photo Credits

• All photographs are courtesy of NASA (National Aeronautics and Space Administration) and JPL (Jet Propulsion Laboratory at Cal Tech) except as noted.

• The photos on pp. 3 and 11 are by Andrew Schuerger.

• The Olympus Mons caldera (pp. 15, 40), Phobos (p. 13), and frozen lake (p. 19) are courtesy of ESA (European Space Agency).

• The dust storm on Earth (p. 18) is courtesy of the Goddard Space Flight Center.

In general, the photos were used as is, but in a few cases slight changes were made for clarity. Many of the photographs used in this book can be downloaded by the public from these websites:

http://origin.mars5.jpl.nasa.gov

http://www.esa.int/SPECIALS/Mars_Express

http://mars.jpl.nasa.gov/mgs

http://www.nasa.gov/centers/kennedy/home/index.html

http://pds.jpl.nasa.gov

http://nssdc.gsfc.nasa.gov/imgcat

http://images.jsc.nasa.gov

http://photojournal.jpl.nasa.gov/index.html

Note: You must use capital letters as shown.

Fact, Fiction, or Future?

The content of this book is mostly factual, with a little fiction and a lot of looking ahead to a possible future. The facts are believed to be correct as of the publication date, but scientific research continues. Updates with new information will be posted on www.LoreenLeedy.com. Below are a few notes about the book's fictional and futuristic content:

• Many of the Mars images were photographed in smaller pieces and assembled later on Earth, and may still have visible seams. A few minor defects were retouched in several photos, and the sky was extended to fill the page. The stars on the book's jacket were painted in.

• As of yet, no humans have traveled to Mars or built colonies. But these events *could* happen....

• Korlin fusion drive spacejets, FlexAble laptops, hoverbots, and gravity boots have not been invented yet (as far as we know). Maybe they'll exist someday, or something similar will.

• The building in the background of p. 3 is the Vehicle Assembly Building at Kennedy Space Center in Florida. It is used for the final assembly of spacecraft such as the Apollo moon rockets and the Space Shuttles before they are rolled out to the launchpad.

• As we finished this book the Spirit and Opportunity rovers were still operational and continued to send new data from Mars to Earth.

• Most people in the United States don't use the metric system for measuring, but scientists and people in many other countries do.

We look forward to a future when people can visit and even live on Mars.

Loreen Leedy
and
Andrew Schuerger

Olympus Mons caldera